IMAGES OF CHANGE

IMAGES OF CHANGE

Paintings on
the *I Ching*

by TERRY MILLER

Edited with commentaries
by HALE THATCHER

E. P. DUTTON & CO., INC.

NEW YORK

The editor and the publishers gratefully acknowledge Princeton University Press for permission to use the quotations from the *I Ching* or *Book of Changes*, the Richard Wilhelm translation rendered into English by Cary F. Baynes (Bollingen Series XIX, 3rd. edition, Princeton, 1967).

The accompanying text for each painting has been drawn from its corresponding hexagram.

Reprinted by permission of Princeton University Press and Routledge & Kegan Paul Ltd., London.

First published, 1976, in the United States by E.P. Dutton & Co., Inc. / All rights reserved under International and Pan-American Copyright Conventions. / No part of this book may be reproduced or transmitted in any form or by any means, electronic or mechanical, including photocopy, recording, or any information storage and retrieval system now known or to be invented, without permission in writing from the publishers, except by a reviewer who wishes to quote brief passages in connection with a review written for inclusion in a magazine, newspaper, or broadcast. / Published simultaneously in Canada by Clarke, Irwin & Company Limited, Toronto and Vancouver. / Printed and bound by Dai Nippon Printing Co., Ltd., Tokyo, Japan. / Library of Congress Catalog Card Number: 75-10079 / ISBN 0-525-13182-5. First Edition

Designed by The Etheredges

For Allan Anderson, teacher of religions

ACKNOWLEDGMENTS

The editor wishes to thank the guardian of the Terry Miller collection, Michael Underhill, who has helped in many ways and has allowed the paintings to be photographed for this book.

Special acknowledgment must go to the teacher of the *I Ching*, Law Yip Sun, in Hong Kong, who did the calligraphy in "orchid leaf" brush style.

Random House, Inc., has given permission to use the quotation from Laotse, drawn from *The Wisdom of Laotse*, translated by Lin Yutang (New York: Modern Library no. 262, 1948, p. 140).

The author would like to further express his thankfulness to the painter Jim Bertram, to Michael Fagan, Demetre Lagios, Cindy Rodugas, H. M. Krohnen, Esq., Henry Poirot, who made it happen, Paul Snyder for photography, and in particular to Judi Yabumoto for her time and assistance in preparing manuscripts.

CONTENTS

APPENDICES

PREFACE

The artist, Terry Miller, based his works on the Wilhelm/Baynes translation of the *I Ching* (published in the Bollingen Series by Princeton University Press). I have therefore quoted from this translation in an attempt to abbreviate or outline some of the basic themes in each hexagram and to relate them to the appropriate paintings without distorting the meaning of the original text. For this purpose I have drawn key phrases and fragments from Book I and Book III and correlated these on the pages opposite to each painting. Some additional words about the illustrations appear at the bottom of each page. The quotations will hopefully reveal some of the symbolic and metaphysical depths fundamental to the paintings and also introduce the *Book of Changes* to those who do not yet know it. I am indebted to Princeton University Press for their kind permission to quote from The Wilhelm/Baynes translation, and I hope that this book of art will serve as an inspirational companion to the *I Ching*.

INTRODUCTION

In reading the *I Ching* we encounter a mystery that can be indirectly known yet not explained. It is an oracle founded upon intuitive laws of chance and at the same time it is systematic and logical. It draws from both the wisdoms of heart and mind and speaks out from the unknown in a quiet, detached voice that nourishes like the water from a bottomless well. It tells of the perpetual changes that animate all life. As an oracle it seems clearer and more infallible than such systems as tea-leaf reading or the Tarot cards. Its structure reflects a higher, supreme organization behind all things. This is conceived as a family of eight primal beings: Father who is heaven, Mother who is earth, the Arousing Son, the Abysmal Son, the Resting Son, and three daughters, the Gentle, the Clinging, and the Joyous. It is the symbolic relationships between these archetypes that define any given situation for a reader. In approaching the *Book of Changes* it is helpful for a reader with some common sense and practice to confront it as though it were a living mind: an intelligence refined, discarnate, ancestral, who continues among us for the sake of our enlightenment.

As a book, it represents the quintessence of Chinese wisdom. It was conceived over the centuries by some of the Orient's most profound seers and thinkers, including Confucius. The *I Ching* forms an enigmatic yet practical system of images, judgments, and revelations that deals with the mechanics of change in space and time. It is an instrument for understanding the processes of change, and by changing it remains unchanging and seems lodged out of time. Like a map it spells out all the rises, declines, and spaces in the landscape of our being. It inspires correct action and warns of pitfalls and dangers each step of the way; and it often exposes to us the seeds of future events as they are developing now, in the present. But more than unraveling the threads of human fate, the *Book of Changes* dwells upon a vast order in the universe, especially as it can be perceived and followed at any moment in the changes of our daily lives. For nothing is too small or too large to reveal the design, the symmetrical network in the tapestry of appearances. As the poet Li Shang-Yin has written, "See it small, and the world can hide in a pinpoint."

To inquire of the oracle we should first form a question and then empty the mind. Through the cryptic act of throwing coins or counting yarrow stalks, we then receive from random patterns, six lines (either firm or yielding) that describe the cosmic architecture of events behind the living moment. The *I Ching* contains in the shapes of its pure lines a model for all the transformations and states of being that exist in nature. The book travels with us in serial time although it is thousands of years old. Wherever we are, our footprints find echoes preserved and given meaning within the text. It is a teacher, guide, and mysterious companion.

But in addition to teaching it also forms a deep reservoir of ideas, metaphors, and symbols that are animate and teeming with the life stuff—a reservoir so deep and vast that it cannot be measured by rules or doctrines. It is a fabulous mine of paradox out of which the fountains of true poetry are born, poetry that transcends its words and flows from the archetypes buried in the personal substrata of mind. Ancient pictures and names for the unknown and sleeping secrets of earth itself are brought out into the conscious light, image after image arises out of nature to create an enlarged, symbolic view of correspondence between ourselves, heaven, and earth. Rivers thread its pages; mountains, craters, great waters, and celestial lights are symbols grounded transparently within the unity of all being—symbols that link the organic and seasonal phases in the world outside to changes within the human psyche. We flow out of ourselves into the rocks and trees to discover parallel laws that govern climates, elements, flora, and fauna. Each detail and particular form in nature focuses the universal order: a single leaf is a window into the stars, and the roots of trees like our veins reveal the rhythmic-circular Tao of change that passes through all things (birth, flowering, decay, death, and rebirth).

The sixty-four hexagrams form constellations of figures that mirror the world, reflecting in the changes of their lines, the separate hours of a universal timepiece. Each one describes an original location for us between the courses of heaven and earth.

In rare, inspired art, Terry Miller creates graphic picture worlds for each hexagram. Where the book arbitrates or speaks, he sees. Entering the psychic levels of the *I Ching*, there in the archives of Asian wisdom, he blends some of his own essence into the shadows of the old traditions, giving them new life. As an artist, he uses the hexagrams as vehicles that levitate over our finite horizons in a sphere of vision that is his own.

It takes much time, traveling through the eye into these delicate landscapes, to perceive the subtlety and distance of their impressions. It is like peering through these thin windows into another world—one related to ours, but filled with all the strangeness of spaces half-remembered from dreams. There are scenes subtle to the point of being almost invisible, in which a drifting surreal calm hangs over the mountains and glass canyons, and ranges of fir slowly fade through the curtains of the horizon. They are filled with the awe and utter insignificance of man in the face of nature's more profound moods. These are atmospheres reaching far back into the primeval origins of the eye, where all is fertile, untouched, rich with power and magic. In the dim aurora of beginnings, in the breeding grounds of the mysteries, ravines crystallize out of mist and panoramas appear suspended on mere strings, dissolving in coves of light—but the visions in his pictures speak for themselves.

There are Taoist influences throughout the artist's motifs, especially the way in which conflicting elements are unified. Below the tranquil surfaces, opposing forces are at work, never dissonant but flowing and quietly unresolved. The repressed violence in plate 17 creates an image of controlled shock, whereas in others the polarized space, economy of form, simplicity, and pure rhythm are blended for meditation. They conceal intensity—one must search for those dynamisms of nature. But they are there, perfected, held in the background, modest yet spectacular (as in plate 14, *Possession in Great Measure*, in which the sun's rays are an avalanche on the thread ends of visibility).

In the size and format of the paintings, as well as in the renderings of the mist cliffs and valleys, an influence can be traced back to those mountain landscapes on some of the silk and bamboo scrolls of the Sung Dynasty. Terry Miller's paintings, however, were not executed in the swift spontaneous brushstrokes that one finds in some of the Chinese scrolls, where lines were dashed out after meditation with the ease of notes rising from a stringed instrument. Rather, these were crafted by Western hands, with the control of a jeweler. They grew out of the void like slow crystals, gathering form within a classical and studied sense of limit: the supreme clarity is calculated and precise as a microscope. At times his lines and shapes, in condensed yet elegant detail, can be compared to the concentration in some of the late fifteenth-century Persian miniatures. But the purpose here is not merely to decorate with crowded arabesques and flourishes of style; instead, he draws a rhythmic blueprint of the moods and forces active in nature, whose evasive outlines are captured not only through the artist's discipline and craft, but also by the freedom he allows his own imagination.

Miller developed his style through subtle transfigurations without regard to the art vogue of today or any other historical convention. The delicate, visionary beauty of these pictures goes beyond time and place. They often allude, as Blake did in his engravings, to currents of pure energy—those light waves, tides, and vibrations that flow invisibly through all matter. (Examples are plate 32, *Duration*, and plate 61, *Inner Truth*, and others.) In plate 17, *Following* (in which lightning appears under the sea), the artist defies physical laws and creates unexpected perceptions and gaps in the mind. But this shifting of realities through the power of metaphor should not be difficult to grasp in an age when negative mass and holes in space are current ideas in physics. These paintings enter the regions of the unconscious, not as random surrealism but as magnifications of a deeper order of things. Their goal is always to illuminate the symbols and phenomena of this world, not merely to record but to discover nature, lifting her with great tenderness into new dimensions that have always been her own, but have been hidden from our eyes.

In recasting the themes of the hexagrams he also captures the outlines of our northwestern coast. There are places in my wanderings through fjords and peninsulas near Caspar and Navarro, California, where I have been struck not only by the stark beauty of a ravine, or a certain series of cliffs carved over the ocean, but something else familiar that seemed to hold me there. I had first seen this place in one of his paintings. He was intimate with water, and at home in the slow trances of mist and fog that climb in whiteness out of the turbulent and ever rocking acres of the sea, where iron shores chiseled by waves diminish, slanting into the north as far as the eye can see. Canyons scalloped with moss and webbed pools are there, and always, dark, brooding, silent, and immense, the wilderness with populations of trees stretches its vast body over hills toward the white solitude of the mountains.

Albion, 1972

PART I

A rainstorm continues not a whole day.
. . . .
Even Nature does not last long (in its utterances),
How much less should human beings?

LAOTSE

1. CH'IEN, THE CREATIVE:

. . . the primal power, which is light-giving,
active, strong, and of the spirit.
. . . its essence is power or energy.
Its image is heaven.
. . . it is the beginning of all things.

This first picture suggests a hieroglyph for the abstract principles of the beginning. The two forces of light and dark meet in simple angular spaces, rather than in a rhythmic sphere as found in the Yin and Yang. In two dimensions, and only in the foreground, we see represented here the pure idea of creation, before it materializes in the world of forms. The light is falling from above. A dark horizontal figure divides the light and by its conspicuous placement therein resembles the number *one* on its side. Then another, larger darkness continues below. This plate is unique in the series. Being abstract, it might appear as a mere pattern, but it represents something the very nature of which is abstract and transcends all that we know on earth.

3

2. K'UN, THE RECEPTIVE:

... the Receptive is that which brings to birth,
that which takes the seed of the heavenly into itself,
and gives to beings their bodily form.

... yielding, devoted ...

It represents nature in contrast to spirit,
earth in contrast to heaven ...

The primal spell has been broken. This landscape of tranquil beauty appears in the familiar three-dimensional space of the outer world. From a ridge in the foreground a single tree bends over the valley. The faint edges of cliffs graduate in perspective through the distance, descending into emptiness below. This deep valley, like the yielding lines in the hexagram itself, opens full of the soft birth mist and stretches away without boundary. Many shapes and forms are concealed in its vast expanse—hazy, opaque, enchanted—the original valley of the womb.

3. CHUN, DIFFICULTY AT THE BEGINNING:

Clouds and thunder . . . teeming, chaotic profusion;
. . . heaven and earth bring forth individual beings.

. . . the firm and the yielding unite for the first time,
and the birth is difficult.

But these difficulties arise from the very profusion
of all that is struggling to attain form.

This first meeting between heaven and earth is depicted as an explosive event.
In a storm the jagged white shaft of light wrinkles the air and tapers away in
patches of haze. Lightning manifests its absolute power in a flash, and its energy
is then absorbed again into the soft translucent clouds. The sky is intense,
dangerous, full of fear and excitement. The electric force of the storm acts as a
catalyst that creates the possibility of a first birth.

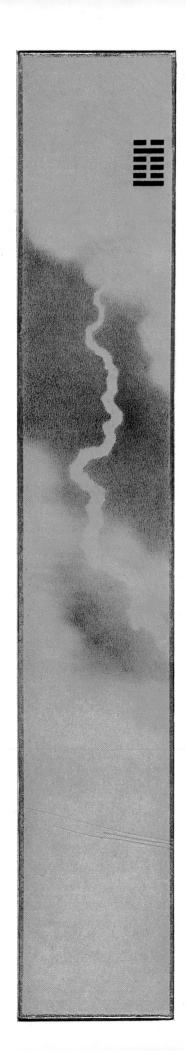

4. MÊNG, YOUTHFUL FOLLY:

. . . the image of inexperienced youth.

> . . . danger at the foot of a mountain.
> Danger and standstill . . .

> YOUTHFUL FOLLY means confusion and
> subsequent enlightenment.

These first pictures announce the themes like the early chords in a symphony.
The natural events that proceed from painting to painting illustrate the laws
of being and the stages of becoming that effect them. Here the undeveloped
time of youth is portrayed by the central placement of a cactus low in the foreground. Its delicate arms point upward. The stones at its base suggest a solid
foundation from which it grows. This early struggling into form after birth is
contrasted with the calm and patience of the ancient mountain behind.

5. HSÜ, WAITING (NOURISHMENT):

Clouds rise up to heaven . . .

. . . it will not be long before rain falls.

All beings have need of nourishment from above. But
the gift of food comes in its own time . . .

The food of rain originates in the heavens where slow, nebulous clouds drift
like soft towers sculptured in air. The white, vertical mass, which dominates
most of the picture's height, is penetrated and broken from the right by thin,
horizontal currents of wind. This contrast in rhythm between the clouds and
the motion of the wind implies a gradual change taking place. This requires
waiting.

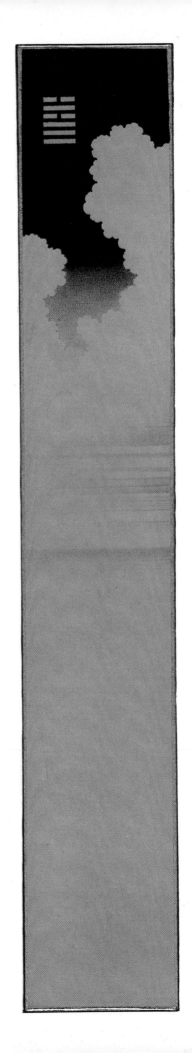

言公

6. SUNG, CONFLICT:

. . . the two halves move away from each other,
giving rise to the idea of conflict.

CONFLICT means not to love.

The two halves, above and below, separate as opposing elements. The sky rises
and the ground sinks, anchored below in modulated lines of ink monochrome.
The hills, flanked by umbral silhouettes of mounds in the distance and shadow
foliage in the foreground, slant in tense and rigid contrast to the open space
above.

This plate (and most of the others) expresses an objective state in nature as
well as a subjective, psychological state in man. It is interesting to compare this
rendering of "conflict" with some of the occult interpretations of shapes seen
in the human aura in persons under pressure or in conflict. (1)

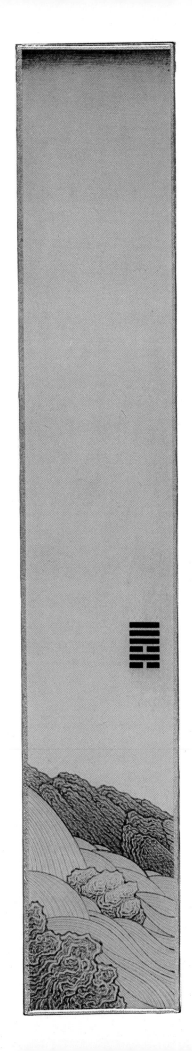

師

7. SHIH, THE ARMY:

In the middle of the earth is water . . .

THE ARMY means mourning.

. . . people are sheltered by their government
as ground water is sheltered by the earth . . .

Here the symbols water, mist, mountain, and moon achieve a lost nocturne of satori. The brushwork is circumspect, delicate, magical, and creates in all a supernatural impression of the night. Below, a black void surrounds the weaving polyphonic rhythms of the water, whose buoyant lines meander out of nothingness, treading space with the clarity of frozen rays. Above, an immense floating gauze of salt mist spreads, opaque, gentle, undefined, drifting on the mountains, where rivers of fog slide under the moon.

ΓΚ

8. PI, HOLDING TOGETHER [UNION]:

The waters on the surface of the earth flow together . . .
uniting . . . joyous.

. . . so should the organization of society show union.

Truth, like a full earthen bowl . . .

The waterfall surges and floods, slicing through stone cliffs, where the listless, dark inertia of rock gives way to its ceaseless motion. Even in the static rocks, many lines in complicated, intricate mazes suggest a sense of urgency and inner motion. These jagged cliffs open like veins through which the jugular river falls toward the sea.

小畜

9. HSIAO CH'U, THE TAMING POWER OF THE SMALL:

The wind restrains the clouds, the rising breath of
the Creative . . . Dense clouds, no rain . . .

. . . a strong element is temporarily held in leash by a
weaker element . . . the power of the shadowy—that restrains,
tames, impedes.

The theme of this picture is wind in the sky . . . Wind, the First Daughter, who
by her gentleness and penetration, restrains the storm-making power in the
heavens. This format of pure space in the lower half of the composition,
horizontal breezes, and clouds assembled above, corresponds to plate 5 (and
others later). But this one focuses on the graceful, sweeping form of the wind
as it emerges from the right in woven layers, like the shapes of tissues and
slender muscular fibers.

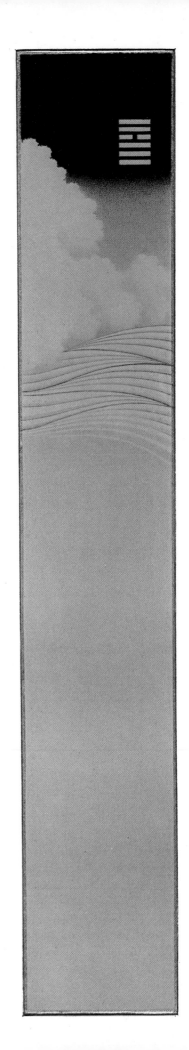

履

10. LÜ, TREADING [CONDUCT]:

The youngest daughter [Lake] walks behind the
father [Heaven].

This shows the difference between high and low . . .

. . . if inner worth forms the criterion of external rank,
people acquiesce and order reigns in society.

In this atmosphere the element water is again deeply charged with the vital
pulsations of life. Lines of hair thickness, not stiff but flowing, resolve in glid-
ing waves. An impressionistic feeling of all that is transitory is achieved here
by subtle variations of tone. Above and below blend softly. The vague miragelike clouds disintegrate on the face of the Joyous Lake, where waters in minute,
ever-churning, interflowing rhythms weave across the mist. It is liquid calligraphy, efflorescence of light and shadow.

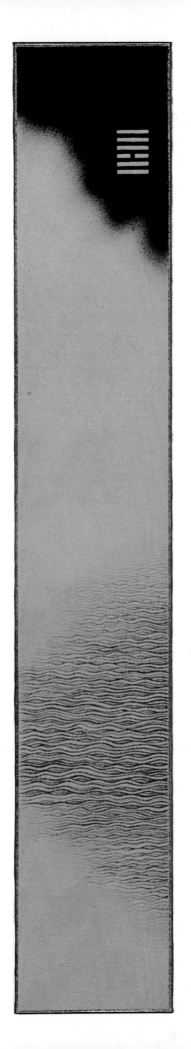

11. T'AI, PEACE:

The small departs,
The great approaches.

. . . the forces of nature prepare the new spring.
. . . their powers unite in deep harmony.
. . . a time in nature when heaven seems to be on earth.

. . . all living things bloom and prosper.

February-March: the maternal, yielding earth receives the birth-giving power of light from above, and all things expand, filling to the zenith.

Under the noon sun, creased edges of a ravine unfold into the slow waters below. From the top right, many rays fan out over a vast panorama. This sun and its mandala of beams should be compared to the subtle rendering in plate 14, *Possession in Great Measure*. Both paintings exhibit a beautiful control of perspective.

23

12. P'I, STANDSTILL [STAGNATION]:

. . . those above are out of union with those below.

Each according to his kind.

This hexagram (*Standstill*) describes the opposite of the preceding one (*Peace*). Here the time of August-September is represented as the beginning of autumn. Heaven and earth grow farther apart. It is the time of decay.

Meticulous clarity of detail continues throughout this landscape. Only a difference in size distinguishes the fore-, mid-, and backgrounds. Each tiny fractioned hill or ridge reveals intricate craftsmanship. Even those far, unfading, faint verges of foothills under the mountain stand out like carvings in crystal.

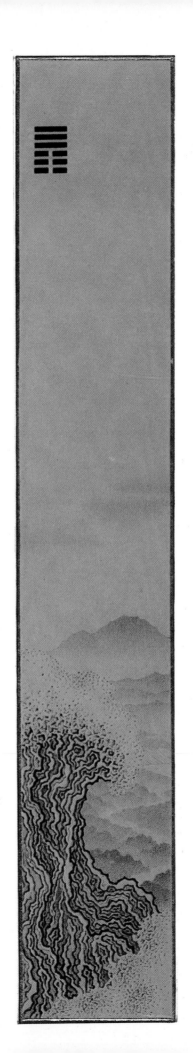

13. T'UNG JEN, FELLOWSHIP WITH MEN:

Just as the luminaries in the sky serve for the
systematic division and arrangement of time,
so human society and all things that really belong
together must be organically arranged.

In a ritual, fire climbs toward heaven, motioning to the greater celestial lights
of sun and stars.

The graceful motion of the flame is rendered evenly, smoothly, with the finish
of polished marble in a sculpture. Its texture, like woven reeds, resembles the
form of water (as in plate 17, *Following*). This similarity in form between the
two (fire and water) implies that opposites are not separate, antagonistic forces,
but are related through mutual dependency—night and day like water and fire
are two manifestations of the same principle.

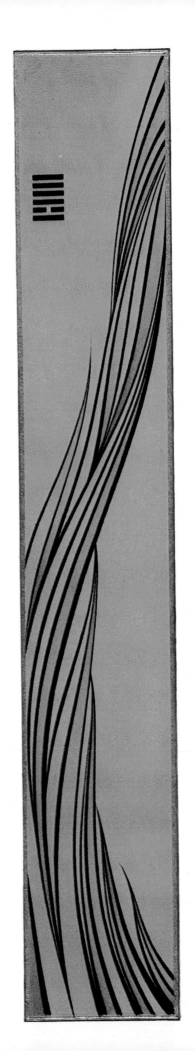

14. TA YU, POSSESSION IN GREAT MEASURE

The sun . . . shedding light over everything on earth,
. . . all things stand out in the light and become manifest.

The overall beauty of this painting creates an impression—an atmosphere of muted tones, a gentle blur of moods that express ineffable relations.

Among labyrinths and contours at the continent's end, five plateaus spread into the distance where the oval sun's globe glows, radiant, yet mysterious and half-hidden in haze. This view was taken from the cliffs and fjords near Caspar on the northern California coastline.

29

言兼

15. CH'IEN, MODESTY:

It is the law of heaven to make fullness empty and
to make full what is modest; when the sun is at its
zenith, it must, according to the law of heaven,
turn toward its setting, and at its nadir it rises
toward a new dawn.

It is the law of earth to alter the full and to
contribute to the modest. High mountains are worn
down by the waters, and the valleys are filled up.

It is the law of fate to undermine what is full and
to prosper the modest. And men also hate fullness
and love the modest.

In this quiet, tranquil scene the domes of hills like many rolling waves represent
restraint and humbleness of character. The nine mounds are evenly patterned
and resemble in design the sections of a stained-glass window. A fraction of
the mountain visible in the foreground makes a strong contrast to the undulat-
ing hills in the background. The "Mountain is the Youngest Son . . . the repre-
sentative of heaven on earth."

豫

16. YÜ, ENTHUSIASM:

Chên is the sound of the thunder that accompanies the movements of reawakening life. This sound is the prototype of music.

> Thus the ancient kings made music
> In order to honor merit,
> And offered it with splendor
> To the Supreme Deity,
> Inviting their ancestors to be present.

Three ridges yield under three bolts of lightning splintering over the hills. The shafts spring unexpectedly from unseen forces in the sky, and in unison, each angular, wiry bolt shakes loose from the clouds. The silhouettes of the oblique ridges, in ink monochrome, slant in two directions.

"When, at the beginning of summer, thunder—electrical energy—comes rushing forth from the earth again, and the first thunderstorm refreshes nature, a prolonged state of tension is resolved. Joy and relief make themselves felt. So too, music has power to ease tension within the heart and to loosen the grip of obscure emotions . . . From immemorial times the inspiring effect of the invisible sound that moves all hearts, and draws them together, has mystified mankind."

17. SUI, FOLLOWING:

In the autumn electricity withdraws into the earth again . . .
Turning inward . . . This gives rise to the idea of following
or being guided by the laws of nature.

Thunder in the middle of the lake indicates times of
darkness and rest.

". . . the image—thunder in its winter rest, not thunder in motion."

Here the sensitive flowing harmonies of water contrast with the stark, hard,
angular style of the lightning. This represents a blending of masculine and feminine elements, for this hexagram is composed of the Youngest Daughter, Tui,
Lake, and the Oldest Son, Chên, Thunder. As shifting dimensions rotate, the
two unite, hence lightning underwater.

35

18. KU, WORK ON WHAT HAS BEEN SPOILED [DECAY]

The wind blows low on the mountain:
The image of DECAY.

. . . here the things of the past come to an end.

The superior man must first remove stagnation . . . as the
wind stirs everything, and [he] must then strengthen
and tranquillize the character of the people, as the
mountain gives tranquillity and nourishment to all
that grows in its vicinity.

Here again the use of space is exquisitely controlled. Large areas of flat space
are given shape, texture, and motion by much smaller areas of contrasting intensity. This spatial quality in the paintings reveals a Taoist influence. For, according to Tao: emptiness, void, nonbeing, and space form the fertile nothingness
from which all forms rise. Here space acquires an unformed, trans-actual substance that is divided and shaped by the ink brush. This particular creation and
many others minimize form to the utmost. Only the vaguest hints distinguish
high and low, near and far. Yet the faint rims of the mountain above, and the
gentle wheat-spires below clearly define the boundaries and size of the landscape. Over the slopes of the mountain feathers of wind stir latent motion in
the blank, unbreathing space.

19. LIN, APPROACH:

Approach means becoming great.

The earth borders upon the lake from above.
  The lake is inexhaustible in depth . . .
  the earth is boundlessly wide, sustaining
  and caring for all creatures on it . . .
  so the sage sustains and cares for all people
  and excludes no part of humanity.

This serene painting conveys a sense of the ancient past. On the other shore clusters of peaks tower out of the mist like touchstones in the void. The crystalline anger of these old volcanoes has been softened by centuries of snow.

Near the bottom the rhythmic currents flow on uninterrupted. Here again the artist "signed his name in water." (2)

20. KUAN, CONTEMPLATION (VIEW):

A great view is above.

Contemplation of the divine meaning underlying the workings
of the universe gives to the man who is called upon to
influence others the means of producing like effects.

A great view is above.

When the wind blows over the earth it goes far and wide,
and the grass must bend to its power.

This plate corresponds to plate 18. Both treat wind and wheat as themes and
both are rendered in a similar style. This one, however, focuses more closely
on the wheat stalks. Also the longer, riper nuggets at the end suggest a later
time of year, September-October. The vertical curving stalks dominate four-
fifths of the painting's height. They bend under horizontal tides of wind brush-
ing through the sky above.

噬 嗑

21. SHIH HO, BITING THROUGH:

Thunder and lightning:

Movement and clarity.

. . . the coming together occurs in the heavens,
whereupon the line of the lightning appears.
. . . it indicates how obstacles are forcibly removed
in nature.

"Energetic biting through overcomes the obstacle that prevents joining of the lips; the storm with its thunder and lightning overcomes the disturbing tension in nature."

The basic format of this one corresponds to plate 51, *The Arousing*. Both pictures describe the subdued violence of lightning in the sky. Here, only a single shaft descends in luminescence. In plate 51, two longer and more dynamic bolts slash through the clouds.

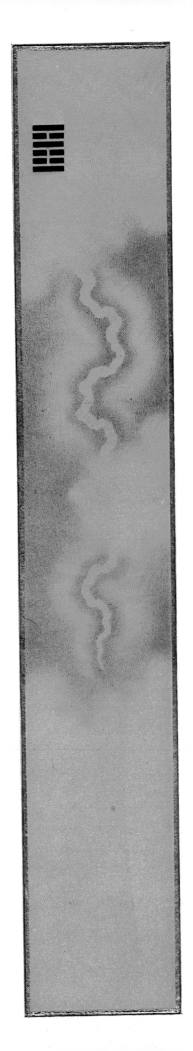

賁

22. PI, GRACE:

. . . fire breaks out of the secret depths of the
earth and, blazing up, illuminates and beautifies
the mountain, the heavenly heights.

The most perfect grace consists not in external
ornamentation but in allowing the original material
to stand forth, beautified by being given form.

The cliffs and shaded ravines, as they slant down through the left margin of the
picture, resemble textures of folded curtains. The treatment of the light-rimmed
rocks in the lower foreground corresponds to sections in plate 15, *Modesty*.
Below, a quiet fire tapers up and illumines the dented, pocked boulders on a
ridge of the mountain. These oval, stylized flames are not so descriptive as those
seen in plate 30, *The Clinging, Fire*. This painting represents a temporary state
of being—Grace as serenity—the tranquil clarity and beauty of "contemplation," which is not to be confused with the Christian concept of Divine Grace.

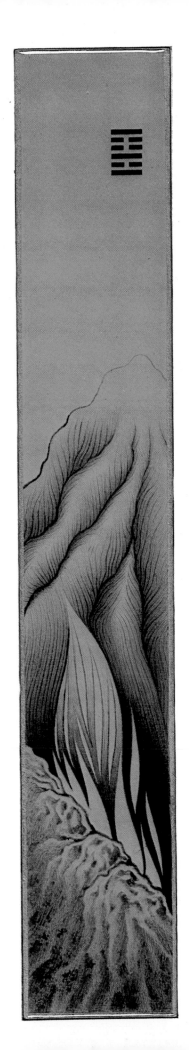

剥

23. PO, SPLITTING APART:

The mountain rests on the earth . . .
Thus those above can ensure their position
Only by giving generously to those below.

This atmosphere focuses upon a dark, concentrated, and intense midground that
is surrounded by pale space above and below. The wiry complex lines translate
motion here even in hard stone. Elements seem to change forms as the painter
twists and blends the metallic strength of stone with an almost equal delicacy to
that of water, softening what is strong, shifting appearances subtly. The minute, complicated modulations of line and shadow produce rhythm. An ancient
presence in these mountains seems to move with all the slow, millennial change
of wrinkles in sages' foreheads.

復

24. FU, RETURN (THE TURNING POINT):

Thunder within the earth:

To and fro goes the way.

The powerful light that has been banished [above] returns.
. . . it returns below.

. . . turning away from the confusion of external things,
turning back to one's inner light. There, in the depths
of the soul, one sees the Divine, the One . . . To know
this One means to know oneself in relation to the cosmic
forces.

"In winter the life energy, symbolized by thunder, the Arousing, is still under-
ground. Movement is just at its beginning . . ."

This plate corresponds to plate 17, in which lightning is seen underwater. Both
hexagrams in the I Ching relate to a time for turning inward and rest, a time
when power and movement are still stirring as potentials under the surface.

The trees near the top of this painting express, again, a sense of life rhythm
within static forms. This is produced by hair-thin lines woven in small, irregular
shapes—wood strands from root to tip of leaf.

无妄

25. WU WANG, INNOCENCE (THE UNEXPECTED):

In springtime when thunder, life energy, begins to
move again under the heavens . . . all beings receive from
the creative activity of nature the childlike innocence
of their original state.

At sea one streak of lightning materializes from the tabular clouds and zigzags
in its descent, piercing the water. Note the subtle chiaroscuro and detail at the
point of contact, where thunder strikes and punctures the ocean. On the glazed
surface a floating, electric patch of light fades among the lateral bands of water.
Shadows define each wave of the currents as they weave symmetrically, gradually, perpetually along the horizon.

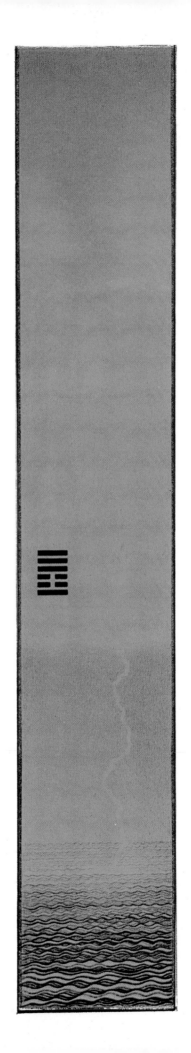

26. TA CH'U, THE TAMING POWER OF THE GREAT:

Heaven within the mountain:

When innocence is present, it is possible to tame.

The Creative [Heaven] below presses powerfully upward,
and Keeping Still [Mountain] above holds it fast . . .

This produces great power . . .

With almost none of the fine detail of the others, this picture conveys a sense of power, weight, and density. The black, undefined strength of the mountain is half-eclipsed and submerged in white fog. Mist permeates three-fourths of this painting. The mysterious haze comes and goes, following its own laws. The slow drifting robe of fog is broken only by a horizontal slit on the lower right.

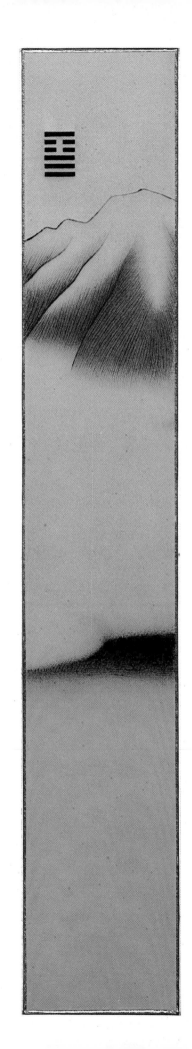

27. I, THE CORNERS OF THE MOUTH (PROVIDING NOURISHMENT):

Turning to the summit
For provision of nourishment
Brings good fortune.
Spying about with sharp eyes
Like a tiger with insatiable craving.
No blame.

This hexagram, 27, *Providing Nourishment*, deals with the time of early spring.

Four miragelike mounds merge into the clouds. Their soft, vague, and uniform texture graduates from pale mist below into silhouettes at the top. In this motif, the idea of infant nourishment is reflected in the suggestive contours of the four breastlike slopes. An overall tone of gentleness permeates the picture.

Midway, slanting across the first cone in the foreground, an angular fork of lightning appears. Lightning belongs here, in the symbolism of the text, for "... in the sign of the Arousing (Thunder) ... the life forces stir again."

大過

28. TA KUO, PREPONDERANCE OF THE GREAT:

A dry poplar sprouts at the root.

. . . the superior man, when he stands alone,
Is unconcerned,
And if he has to renounce the world,
He is undaunted.

This interpretation of a tree is unique in the series. Except for the plume or flamelike outlines of wind in the lower right corner, this painting is simply a graphic still life. Layers of bark wind up the cylinder of the trunk as it bends slightly to the left under pyramids of leaves.

In format the originals resemble scrolls. Each is fourteen inches high and two and one half inches wide. But they are considerably larger (three feet high and twelve inches wide) with matting and with the artist's handmade wooden frames around them.

坎

29. K'AN, THE ABYSMAL (WATER):

In man's world *K'an* represents the heart, the soul
locked up within the body, the principle of light
inclosed in the dark . . . like water in a ravine . . .
It flows on and on . . . it goes through dangerous places . . .
and nothing can make it lose its own essential nature.
It remains true to itself under all conditions.

This is a concentrated masterpiece of Miller's line style. The intricate banks of the ravine, tangled with roots, descend sharply into labyrinths where the river swerves. The tight, angular tapestry of lines on the sides of the channel is contrasted with the graceful abandon of the water as it flows, drawing its fluid signature through the depths. Above, the soft, moss-pillowed tops of the canyon fade into haze.

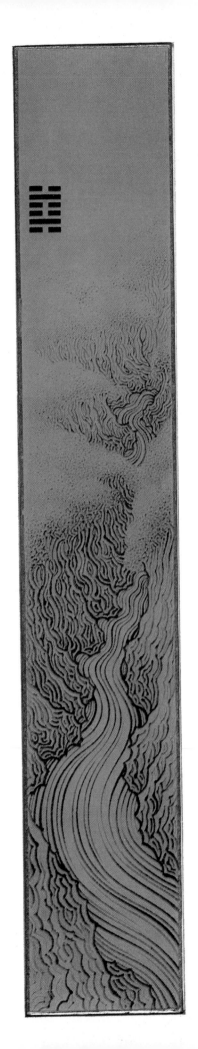

離

30. LI, THE CLINGING (FIRE):

THE CLINGING is directed upward.

Fire has no definite form but clings to the burning
object and thus is bright. As water pours down from
heaven, so fire flames up from the earth.

> . . . Li stands for nature in its radiance . . . and
> represents the summer sun,
> which illumines all earthly things.

Fire, earth's only light,
A soft and desperate hand
Reaching for the sun.

PART II

31. HSIEN, INFLUENCE (WOOING):

After there are heaven and earth, there are the
individual things.

　　　After individual things have come into being,
there are the two sexes.

. . . Tui, the youngest daughter . . . joyousness,
its image is the lake.

. . . Kên, the youngest son . . . keeping still,
its image is the mountain.

. . . lake gives of its moisture to the mountain;
the mountain collects clouds, which feed the lake.

The forces of the two stimulate and respond to
each other, so that they unite.

This hexagram, dealing with the "mutual attraction" between opposites, begins
Part II of the *I Ching*.

Motion in this painting pivots on the peaks of the mountains. Above, clouds
angle subtly toward the farthest summit, and similarly below, the rippling
edges of coastal wharves rise obliquely toward their peaks.

This plate exhibits a range of contrasting linear styles: the currents, with thin
curling strands of water, are braided in a retreat toward the forceful and rugged
delineations of the cliffs. A floating belt of fog obscures their meeting.

32. HÊNG, DURATION:

Thunder and wind:

Their combined action imparts duration to both.

The hexagram represents . . . marriage as the enduring union of the sexes.

Heavenly bodies exemplify duration. They move in their fixed orbits, and because of this their light-giving power endures.

Here we see a synthesis between visual elements that appeared in separate pictures earlier in the series. The lightning shaft, this single white river of fire, is seen whenever the First Son, Thunder, belongs in a hexagram (e.g. plate 3). Also, the motion of pure wind, as portrayed in these plunging, curved, and linear stratifications of air, first appeared in plate 9, *The Taming Power of the Small*. These two images when fused create intense movement. A vertical flash of lightning crosses the path of the invisible being of the wind.

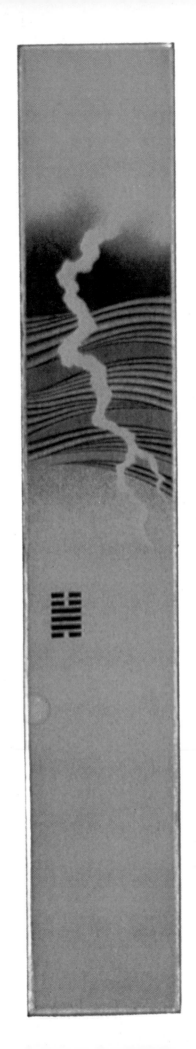

33. TUN, RETREAT:

The power of the dark is ascending. The light
retreats to security, so that the dark cannot encroach
upon it. . . . retreat is a sign of strength.

The strength of this mountain seems almost exaggerated by being concealed by
mist. The floating haze, in its very obscurity, reveals a threshold between the
seen and the unseen. Colors, textures, and shapes are muted in the dense mist
as it clings to, absorbs, and changes the contours of the known.

Each hexagram relates an inner state of being as well as a symbol in the outer
world. Some theories of Impressionism say that depth is more apparent in things
when the surfaces are blurred. The internal meaning reflected in this atmosphere, and in most of the others, can be further illuminated by what Gerard
Manley Hopkins called "inscape"—the "outward reflection of the inner nature
of a thing." (3)

34. TA CHUANG, THE POWER OF THE GREAT:

Thunder—electrical energy—mounts upward in the spring.

. . . a time when inner worth mounts with great force
and comes to power.

A change in the style of lightning is evident here. The picture expresses the
pure idea of principle of the light force in heaven, rather than a graphic representation of its falling to earth. The shaft appears to be moving upward, which
is in keeping with the movement in the hexagram where four strong Yang lines
enter from below and ascend upward with force.

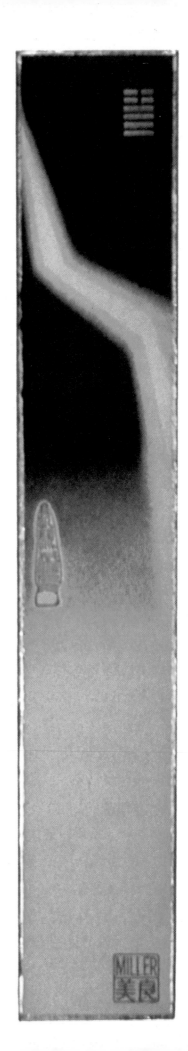

35. CHIN, PROGRESS:

Progress means expansion.

. . . the sun rising . . .

    Clarity rises high over the earth.
    Devoted, and clinging to this great clarity,
    the weak progresses and goes upward.

A time of rapid and easy progress is represented here in the surrealistic matrix of a forest. Voluptuous, veined pillars of wood arch through the sky. The forms of the earth are expanding. Note the remarkable linear clarity of the trunks and the vague sprays of leaves at their tops. Above, the black halo of the sun spins, fringed with electric fuzz.

73

明夷

36. MING I, DARKENING OF THE LIGHT:

Here the sun has sunk under the earth . . .

Here the Lord of Light is in a subordinate place
and is wounded by the Lord of Darkness.
But the injury is not fatal . . .

> "In adversity it furthers one to be persevering":
> this means veiling one's light.

This painting expresses a magnificent gloom. Though *Darkening of the Light* is not interpreted as a productive or positive state, it nevertheless reflects a condition of doubt—an emotional interior or human inscape with which all are familiar. One is drawn into this scene by the powerful magnet of despair. A profound sadness and oppression hangs over the many dark mounds, assembled there like the rusting shrines of the ancestors, unknown and resigned to black oblivion.

37. CHIA JÊN, THE FAMILY [THE CLAN]:

[The] positions of man and woman correspond
with the relative positions of heaven and earth . . .

THE FAMILY is society in embryo . . .

THE FAMILY shows the laws operative within the household
that, transferred to outside life, keep the state
and the world in order.

This motif of flame appears throughout the series as a representation of *Li, The Clinging, Fire.*

"The influence that goes out from within the family is represented by the symbol of the wind created by fire."

In this composition emphasis lies upon the graceful simplicity of the fire. In slender, vertical curves its delicate flames entwine, rising in unison like plumes or ribbons braided around the naked body of a fire.

睽

38. K'UEI, OPPOSITION:

OPPOSITION means estrangement.

Fire flames upward, water seeps downward: when they are quiescent, their movements can unite; when they are in motion, they draw farther and farther apart.

. . . [But] opposition is actually the natural prerequisite for union.

This hexagram is composed of Li, the Second Daughter, and Tui, Lake, the Youngest Daughter. (Fire and water) ". . . These two movements are in direct contrast."

"In general, opposition appears as an obstruction, but when it represents polarity within a comprehensive whole, it has also its useful and important functions. The oppositions of heaven and earth, spirit and nature, man and woman, when reconciled, bring about the creation and reproduction of life."

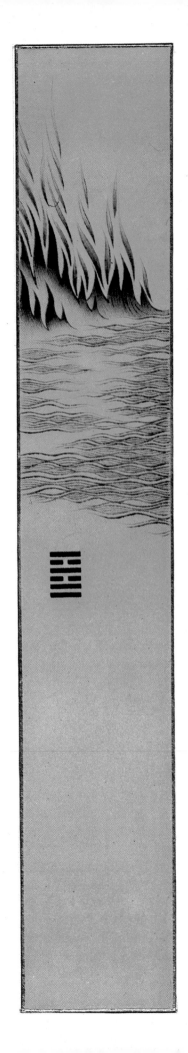

39. CHIEN, OBSTRUCTION:

Water on the top of a mountain cannot flow down
in accordance with its nature, because rocks hinder it.
It must stand still. This causes it to increase,
and the inner accumulation finally becomes so great
that it overflows the barriers. The way of overcoming
obstacles lies in turning inward and raising one's own
being to a higher level.

The theme of this plate is water on the mountain, and how through obstruction
it yields, turns inward, and accumulates until finally it breaks through its
barriers.

The treatment of the rocks and water here compares to scenes in some of Van
Gogh's landscapes, the same uncontrollable life pulse, the same living force
twists and weaves these dense, concentrated shapes with a power that animates
them. In this picture the inner magnetic tensions in the forms of both rock
and water correspond. This suggests that the forms of nature are transparent
and that the same universal energy is active in each.

81

解

40. HSIEH, DELIVERANCE:

Thunder . . . has penetrated the rain clouds.
There is release from tension. The thunderstorm breaks,
and the whole of nature breathes freely again.

The hinderance is past . . .

. . . movement brings deliverance from danger.

The obstacles and danger specified in the last two hexagrams are here resolved.

"Just as rain relieves atmospheric tension, making all the buds burst open, so a time of deliverance from burdensome pressure has a liberating and stimulating effect on life."

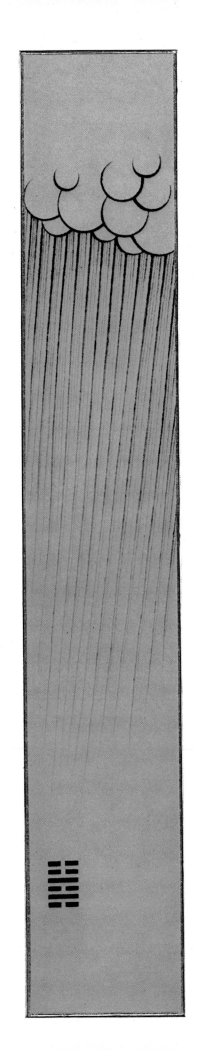

掲

41. SUN, DECREASE:

. . . the instincts drown the heart like the depths
of a lake.

What is below is decreased to the benefit of what is
above.

One may use two small bowls for the sacrifice..

Decrease: "One must draw on the strength of the inner attitude to compensate
for what is lacking in externals . . ."

Mountains buried in shadow. Petals of darkness oppress the waters. The stone
chest of the mountain, holding light, rising absolute over the lake below, is
then obscured in a negative abyss of loss and inertia.

42. I, INCREASE:

The fact that continuous decrease finally leads to a change
into its opposite, increase, lies in the course of nature,
as can be perceived in the waning and waxing of the moon
and in all of the regularly recurring processes of nature.

The time of INCREASE does not endure . . .

When [a man] discovers good in others, he should imitate
it and thus make everything on earth his own.

Although in a vertical format, this plate should be viewed on its side, this hexagram ☳☴ is the inverse of the preceding one ☶☱ . In plate 41 movement
was oppressive and directed downward. Here both wind and thunder represent
motion upward into the sky. The angular, abstract design for lightning is
penetrated by gentle hairlike strands of wind.

"This time resembles that of the marriage of heaven and earth, when the earth
partakes of the creative power of heaven, forming and bringing forth living
beings."

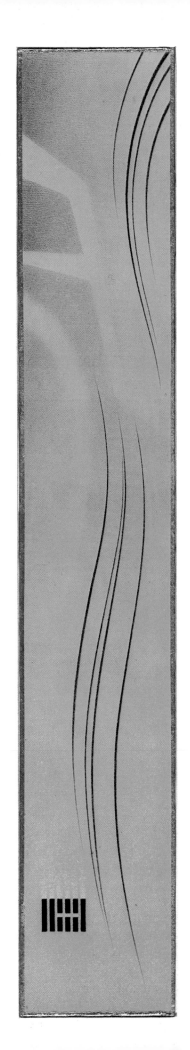

43. KUAI, BREAK-THROUGH (RESOLUTENESS):

The lake has evaporated and its waters are gathering high in the heavens as mist and clouds: this points to an imminent break-through, in which the water will come down again as rain.

... all gathering is followed by dispersion.

This hexagram like plate 10, *Treading*, depicts the Father, Heaven, and the Youngest Daughter, Lake. But here heaven is below the lake. In this atmosphere, through a marvelous shifting of dimensions, high and low change places. In a single plane we see elevations blended. The clouds descend underwater, and water, still in its horizontal, flat-lake state, rises into the sky. The currents are formed by thin, precise lines woven like threads of silk into the shapes of waves. This plate and plate 10 are both examples of the artist's supreme treatment of water and cloud.

44. KOU, COMING TO MEET:

. . . the moment when the earthly force enters
and the heavenly force is at its height
in the fifth month—all things unfold . . .

. . . the time of the meeting of the light with the dark.

Here, as in plate 9, *The Taming Power of the Small,* the Father is seen with the First Daughter, The Gentle, Wind. Here the primeval power of heaven, detached among the altitudes and unknown spaces above, is lured by winds below.

The rocking, topsy-turvy waves of wind, in folded, woven layers, portray a turbulent time when the feminine principle takes the initiative, and in rising after power, first encounters the spacious depths of heaven above.

45. TS'UI [MASSING]:

Over the earth, the lake:
The image of GATHERING TOGETHER

When creatures meet one another, they mass . . .
There are secret forces at work, leading together
those who belong together.

To bring great offerings creates good fortune.

The cliffs descend on a diagonal axis from right to left. Lines mingle and petrify in a surreal landscape of spires, scalloped peaks, and ledges. Note the unique effect of the ridges haloed with light. Here the artist captured the spirits of the mountains, massed together. The hard, rough substance of jagged rocks in the ravines below, like a sculpture, is contrasted with the remote music of the waters above.

升

46. SHÊNG, PUSHING UPWARD:

Within the earth, wood grows . . . steady,
imperceptible progress . . .

. . . wood draws strength for its upward push from the root,
which in itself is in the lowest place . . .

The pushing upward is made possible not by violence
but by modesty and adaptability.

The unusual format of this painting is structured around the empty space in
the center, where an anonymous plant subtly dominates the view from below.
The eye is led into emptiness from two directions: above, the oval leaves and
the webbed contours of a branch point downward; at the bottom, a close-up of
tangled vines and leaf clusters rises into space along the needles of a single
plant. The theme of the hexagram is emphasized by its six spines pushing
upward.

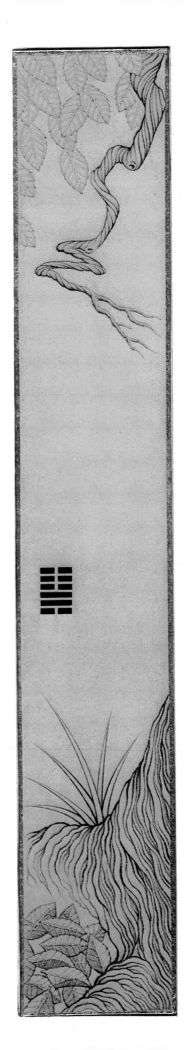

47. K'UN, OPPRESSION (EXHAUSTION):

"One strays into a gloomy valley."

When the water has flowed out below,
the lake must dry up and become exhausted.

> OPPRESSION is the test of character.
> OPPRESSION leads to perplexity and thereby to success.

From the veined foothills and slopes, nebulous linear networks crystallize through a hollow canyon. This picture suggests the emptiness of vast, desolate valleys in the desert, where chasms, emptied by ancient rains and wind, yawn into blank space. The blistered ridges crumble to the floors below, and rest there in the powdered finality of sand.

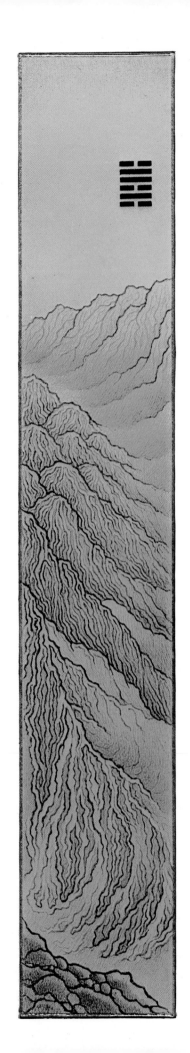

48. CHING, THE WELL:

The well itself does not change, yet through the water that is drawn from it, it exerts a far-reaching influence.

The well nourishes and is not exhausted.

And every human being can draw . . . from the inexhaustible wellspring of the divine in man's nature.

The text for this hexagram and similarly for hexagram 50, *The Caldron*, shows the realized purpose at work throughout the *I Ching*, which is "an inexhaustible dispensing of nourishment."

This placid, graphic still life illustrates the symbols in the hexagram; the bucket, rope, well, and tree are all symbolic objects and carry deeper meanings in relation to the idea of Truth as Water.

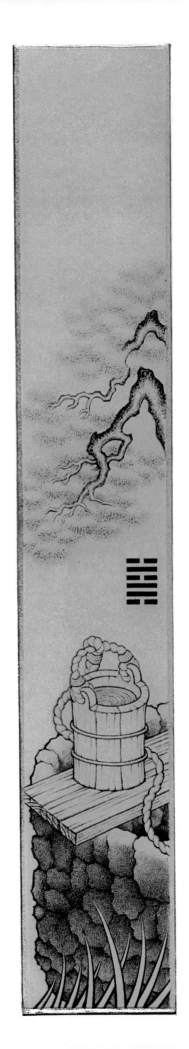

49. KO, REVOLUTION (MOLTING):

Fire in the lake: the image of REVOLUTION.

> Fire below and lake above combat and destroy each other.
> So too in the course of the year a combat takes place be-
> tween the forces of light and the forces of darkness, even-
> tuating in the revolution of the seasons.

As revolutions in nature take place according to fixed laws
and thus give rise to the cycle of the year,
so political revolutions . . . must follow definite laws.

In this plate we see again a juxtaposition of high and low—dimensions overlap
and elements change places. Underwater, the flames leap up, enclosed in a
ghostlike envelope of light. This hexagram shows the inverse of the images in
plate 38, *Opposition*, where the fire is over the water instead of below it.

"The influences are in actual conflict . . . Fire in the lake causes a revolution.
The water puts out the fire, and the fire makes the water evaporate."

50. TING, THE CALDRON:

Here it is the wood that serves as nourishment for the flame, the spirit. All that is visible must grow beyond itself, extend into the realm of the invisible. Thereby it receives its true consecration and clarity and takes firm root in the cosmic order.

The theme here is nourishment. *The Caldron* was originally a bronze vessel for preparing holy food that was used in sacrifices in the temple of the ancestors. Fire heats and cooks the food in the Caldron.

The rendering of the flames in this painting corresponds to plate 37. Both pictures exhibit a similar body of fire as it curls and rises into a single strand of light.

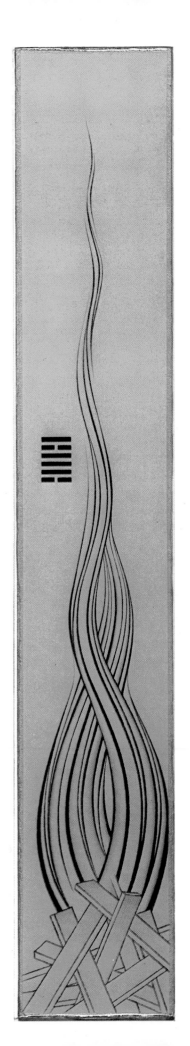

51. CHÊN, THE AROUSING (SHOCK, THUNDER):

Thunder repeated: the image of SHOCK.

The shock of continuing thunder brings fear
and trembling.

. . . Chên represents the eldest son, who seizes rule
with energy and power . . . This movement is so violent
that it arouses terror.

. . . Chên means the coming forth of God in the spring
and also the reawakening of the life-force, which stirs
again from below.

The lightning-bolt motif is carried to perfection here. In vertical descent, two
parallel flashes split and singe the air with all the force of a heightened yet
momentary revelation. Unleashed from the clouds, the power of a great birth
reveals itself. The purified, restless energy of double thunder ushers in the new
spring. In our Western myths this heavenly fire was called the Hammer of
Thor or Zeus's Rod, and was also a powerful manifestation of Jupiter, Jehovah,
El, and many other gods.

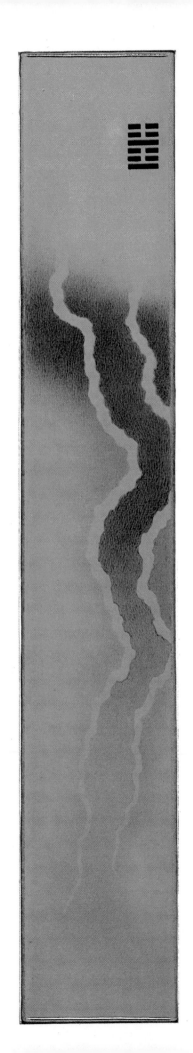

52. KÊN, KEEPING STILL (MOUNTAIN):

Mountains standing close together:

The image of this hexagram is the mountain, the youngest son of heaven and earth.

It is the mysterious place where all things begin and end, where death and birth pass one into the other.

In many ways this picture is the antithesis of the preceding one, which dealt with vital and spontaneous power. Here "movement has come to its normal end." This hexagram "turns upon the problem of achieving a quiet heart."

Here six mountains represent the six lines in the hexagram. The interplay of subtle shadings produces a view of ranges and towering peaks hypnotic with mist. The silent, still eyes of these perennial mountains, tranquil and sublime, witness the traffic of all beings—all that comes to be and passes away.

漸

53. CHIEN, DEVELOPMENT (GRADUAL PROGRESS):

A tree on a mountain develops slowly according to
the law of its being and consequently stands
firmly rooted.

Gentleness that is adaptable, but at the same time
penetrating, is the outer form that should proceed
from inner calm.

"The tree on the mountain is visible from afar, and its development influences
the landscape of the entire region. It does not shoot up like a swamp plant; its
growth proceeds gradually." *Gradual Progress* is concerned with the meaning
of *perseverance*.

Here, among concentrated shapes anchored in the lower fourth of the picture,
a rugged tree stands on a steep incline. Its roots taper into the light-rimmed
slopes of the mountain, as if petrified, and are identical with the contours of
the stone surroundings. The tree is rooted there by pure endurance; nothing
can shake it loose.

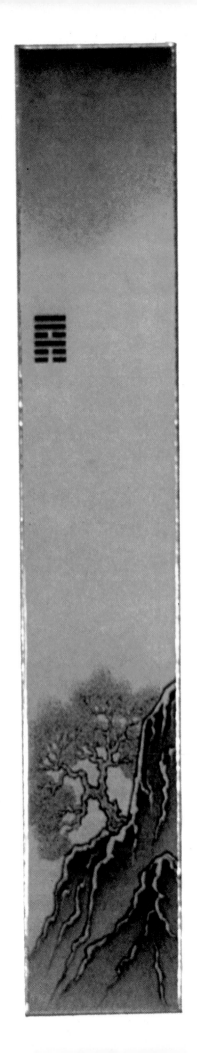

歸妹

54. KUEI MEI, THE MARRYING MAIDEN:

Thunder stirs the water of the lake,
which follows it in shimmering waves.

Affection . . . is of the greatest importance
in all relationships in the world.

This masterpiece on the themes of Thunder and Water reflects the artist's oracular control of imagination. The vision unfolds out across the sea from a rock beach. Again we find the intricate, musical craftsmanship of the tides, where slopes of waves swell, whisper, and weave their thin blue chords like notes from violins. Three strings of lightning interrupt the flowing currents and dent the sea, turning the waters into fire. The ocean is sheeted with light. In soft explosions a glasslike sheen spreads into the distance toward black ridges on the far horizon.

This atmosphere greatly magnifies the visual themes in plate 25, *Innocence*, in which only a single lightning bolt punctures the sea.

55. FÊNG, ABUNDANCE [FULLNESS]

Both thunder and lightning come:
The image of ABUNDANCE.

One should give light to the whole world.

But such a time . . . also carries hidden dangers.
For according to the universal law of events,
every increase is followed by decrease, and
all fullness is followed by emptiness.

This plate traces a shorthand variation in the style of lightning. It is more like the blueprint or the negative of an idea. This electrical abstraction, in stark, black-and-white patterns, suggests the unexpected and sudden way in which a time of abundance may arrive.

旅

56. LÜ, THE WANDERER:

Fire does not linger on the mountain,
but passes on rapidly.

Strange lands and separation
are the wanderer's lot. . . . his home is the road.

The archetypal Chinese sage is often portrayed as either the hermit or the wanderer. It sometimes occurred in the lives of the great sages (those who were not already travelers) that a time of easy and uninhibited wandering opened up new possibilities for absorption into the absolute. Lao Tzu, Chuang Tzu, Lieh Tzu, and even Confucius, among others were all at one time or another wanderers.

Through personal freedom and spontaneity on the road the wanderer explores random loopholes in the chain of events, seeking mystical unity through direct experience rather than through the labor of ideas.

> "All the fish needs
>   Is to get lost in water.
>   All man needs is to get lost
> In Tao." (4)

57. SUN, THE GENTLE (THE PENETRATING, WIND):

Winds following one upon the other:

It is the eldest daughter . . . gentleness,
which penetrates like the wind . . .

Penetration produces gradual and inconspicuous effects.

Herein lies the power of influence.

It means the flowing of beings into their forms,
it means baptism and giving life.

There is a legend of a monk, living alone in the forest, who became enchanted with the laughter of the wind. One day he tried to capture it in a clay jar. He waited until dusk in the top of a tree, and when the wind came he trapped it for an instant, but was lifted up, carried through the sky, and could only return to earth by releasing the flying jar.

This picture should be viewed sideways, so that the broken bottom line of the hexagram appears below the other lines. The swerving fibers form a horizontal S-shaped design that indicates rhythm and motion: the pure quintessence of the Gentle Wind.

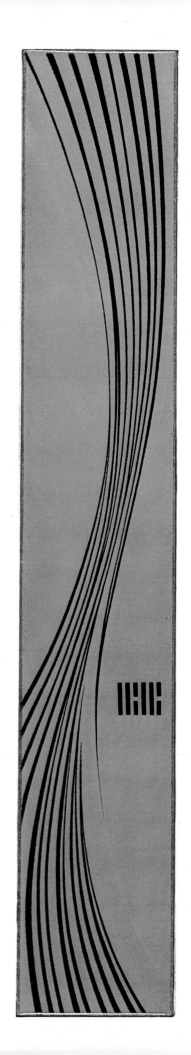

58. TUI, THE JOYOUS (LAKE):

The JOYOUS means pleasure.

. . . Tui denotes the youngest daughter . . . the smiling lake
. . . which rejoices and refreshes all living things.

. . . they are led to take all hardships upon themselves
willingly, and if need be will not shun death itself,
so great is the power of joy over men.

LAGOONS

Eternity, lake upon lake,
Silence of processional flows,
Unsounded, vast, where worlds anchor
Fleet upon the never bottom,
Subterranean Dynasty.

Her fluid waist emerges from the blue,
Drifting on a shore of symbols.
The confessions that her flesh casts thin
Transparent over water, rocks, and ponds
Like moon reflections stirred away by wind.

Desire and dream, those floating shapes,
Moment islands in the harbor of my arms.
What do the rings say? Ever wider, blue:

The circles of my sense's waves rippling
Like how many lives before and after?
Smiles from the being of the water.

59. HUAN, DISPERSION [DISSOLUTION]:

Wind blowing over water disperses it, dissolving it
into foam and mist. . . . indicating
the breaking up of ice and rigidity.

As against this process of breaking up, the task
of reuniting presents itself. . . .

Religious forces are needed to overcome the egotism
that divides men.

The theme of the hexagram is the *Dispersion* or scattering that follows joy.

In this picture we see perhaps the most rhythmic expression of Wind and
Water in the entire series. The rocking waters respond to the slight flourish of
wind above. Traces of its motion are hinted by slender quill strokes through
the sky. But the sea below reflects another quality of silent depth under the
commotion of the waves, immobile, brooding, unknown—the darkness of liquid
marble and jade.

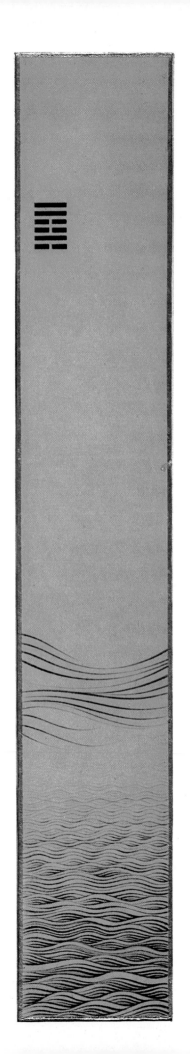

60. CHIEH, LIMITATION:

Water is inexhaustible. A lake can contain
only a definite amount of the infinite quantity
of water . . .

When more water comes into it, it overflows.

Unlimited possibilities are not suited to man;
if they existed, his life would only dissolve
in the boundless.

LIMITATION means stopping.

"The Chinese word for limitation really denotes the joints that divide a bamboo
stalk."

Here the textures of rock, water, and foliage blend like the threads of a hanging
tapestry and create a strong falling motion. A burst of light occurs at the point
where flowing tissues of the waterfall strike the lake, and glazed shimmerings
of illumination continue spreading across the surface.

61. CHUNG FU, INNER TRUTH:

Wind stirs water by penetrating it.
Thus visible effects of the invisible manifest themselves.
It furthers one to cross the great water.

The visual themes in plate 59, *Dispersion*, are magnified in this atmosphere, but here the aerial outlines of breezes unfold high over the mountain. The rippling water fleets below are also stirred by the wind. Meticulous waves mingle and churn through the lake. Even the faintest lines, deep in mist, sustain their motion.

小過

62. HSIAO KUO, PREPONDERANCE OF THE SMALL:

PREPONDERANCE OF THE SMALL is like a bird;
the danger for it lies in mounting too high
and losing the ground under its feet.

"When the strong elements within preponderate, they necessarily enforce their
will. This creates struggle and exceptional conditions in general."

In this picture the Arousing-Thunder motif is expressed in a single flash of light
that lashes down from the drifting clouds, like the snap of a whip, striking the
top of the first peak. Black ridges in the foreground absorb its power in silence
and nonaction. Curtains of fog shroud the lower zones of the mountain.

既濟

63. CHI CHI, AFTER COMPLETION:

. . . fire and water counteract each other,
whereby an equilibrium is created . . . it is just when
perfect equilibrium has been reached that any movement
may cause order to revert to disorder.

This picture is one where conflicting natural elements (Water and Fire) are symbolized as forces that in their very opposition effect a kind of balance. Falling shafts of rain sweep through the fire, and curved, fish-shaped fragments of flame break away, rising into the water.

未濟

64. WEI CHI, BEFORE COMPLETION:

. . . the sun shines forth in redoubled beauty after rain . . .

The hexagram BEFORE COMPLETION represents a transition from chaos to order . . . [and] a parallel to spring, which leads out of winter's stagnation into the fruitful time of summer.

It points to the fact that every end contains a new beginning.

This plate forms a synthesis of four graphic themes that were treated separately in earlier pictures of the series. The mandala of the sun (plate 14), the dark maternal mounds (plate 27), the mist (plate 17), and the rhythmic threads of the water (plate 43) are all blended into an atmosphere of magic and fleeting depth. It is appropriate to find, for the final chapter in the I Ching, these collected motifs polished into a mirror that reflects a partial view back through the labyrinth of the hexagrams.

APPENDICES

THE SIXTY-FIFTH PAINTING

The word *sansui* in both Japanese and Chinese means landscape or simply mountain and water—"assuming that in a perfect landscape painting or poem there must occur both the upheaval of form and the contrast, or softening of it by alluvial motion." (5)

With this final landscape Miller carried his series of pictures one step beyond the themes and images in the hexagrams of the *I Ching* (which go only to 64). He finished this one for his own reasons. The ironic purity of this painting, with flowers in the foreground over the flowing water currents and sharp mountains, constitutes the last expression of his life.

NOTES

1. Annie Besant, *Thought Forms* (Wheaton, Ill.: The Theosophical Publishing House, abridged 1969).

2. Quote from John Keats's epitaph.

3. W. A. M. Peters, S.J., *Gerard Manley Hopkins: A Critical Essay Towards the Understanding of his Poetry* (New York: Oxford University Press, 1948).

4. Thomas Merton, *The Way of Chuang Tzu* (New York: New Directions [NDP276], 1969), p. 65.

5. Ernest Fenollosa, *Epochs of Chinese and Japanese Art*, Vol. 1 (New York: Dover Publications, 1963).

BIOGRAPHIES

THE ARTIST

Terry Miller was born on September 17, 1939, in Portland, Oregon. He studied art in Oakland. These sixty-five paintings were realized in the area of Caspar, Navarro, and Mendocino, California, from 1966 to 1970. His pictures were achieved with a fine one-hair brush and pen on rice paper, finished in lacquer, and then mounted in handmade frames. Miller was thirty-one years old when he completed them. As an artist, he was entirely unknown outside of friends and painters in this area. These paintings were the final expression of his life—a work from which he never returned.

THE AUTHOR

Hale Thatcher was born in January 1945, in Saint Louis, Missouri, of English and Cherokee background. He has traveled widely in Africa and the Middle East. He is a translations editor for the San Francisco poetry review *Isthmus*, and is the author of two books of poems, *Moons and Water Rocks* (1970) and *Shadow Pools* (1974), and has also written several plays.